REMEMBER THE MIRACLES

See back of book for list of National Distributors.

Concept development, editing, design and production by CWR.

Illustrations: Jonathan Lee

Printed in England by Linney Print

ISBN 1-85345-361-7

Remember When Jesus Fed 5,000 People

Written and illustrated by Jonathan Lee

The end of the school day had come and the children were looking forward
to their tea. But before they went home, Mrs Phips had an amazing story to
tell them of when Jesus fed over 5,000 people. She cleared her throat,
'Uh hem,' and began to read . . .

One day, Jesus went up to a mountain with His disciples. All day He had been healing people who were unwell and as He looked out He could see a great multitude coming towards Him. They had followed Him because of His wonderful miracles.

Jesus began to teach the people about God's kingdom. After a while Jesus could see that they were all very hungry and without food, so He asked one of His disciples, Philip, 'Where shall we get some food from?'

Of course, Jesus being all-loving and powerful knew how He would feed them, but Philip was puzzled ...

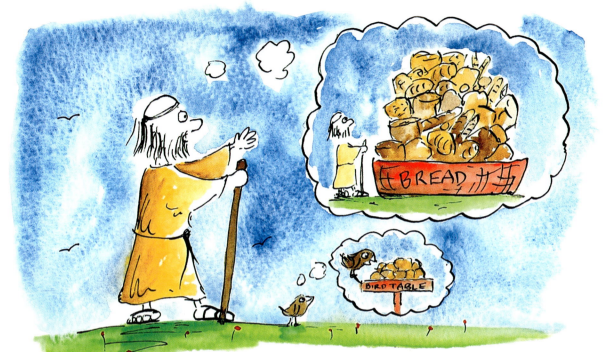

'Even if we had 200 pennies worth of bread we wouldn't have enough for even a bite each,' said Philip.

But just then Andrew, the brother of Simon Peter, found somebody very important holding something very precious . . .

'There is a boy here,' declared Andrew, 'who has five loaves and two small fishes, but that won't feed many people!'

Andrew did not realise that Jesus had a wonderful plan, which was about to be put into action . . .

'Make the people sit down,' Jesus told the disciples.

And so on the green grass surrounding the mountain sat over 5,000 very hungry people in groups of 50 and 100.

Jesus took the five loaves and two fishes and gave thanks to God. He then gave them to His disciples to give to the people.

Everybody was full up! The five loaves and two fishes just seemed to go on and on, lasting until not one more bite could be eaten.

Jesus told the disciples to gather up all the fragments of food that remained. From this great feast they gathered twelve baskets full of leftover bread and fish . . .

All the people that saw how Jesus fed so many with so little were amazed and talked among themselves saying, 'This is truly the Prophet we have been waiting for.'

When Jesus saw that they wanted to make Him a king He left them and went up a mountain again alone to pray to His Father in heaven. It was not long before Jesus had to perform another miracle to rescue His disciples from a raging stormy sea . . .

'But that's another story,' said Mrs Phips as she closed the
book. Before she could ask the class a question about what was
read, a little girl called Isabel put her hand up to ask Mrs Phips . . .

'Why did Jesus take a little boy's lunch to feed the people, surely that's a bit unfair?'

Mrs Phips did not know what to say, but she knew what Isabel was thinking so she answered, 'Well Isabel, I'm sure the boy did eat an[d] had plenty for himself, but there is a big lesson we can learn from thi[s] wonderful miracle . . .

← Everybody else!

Very long table!

. . . Imagine you had to feed the whole school with yo[u]

...nch and they were all very hungry – it would not be easy! . . . .

But you see, the little boy gave what little he had to Jesus who used it in a remarkable and wonderful way. Just as that boy had been given his lunch, a gift, we too have been given many gifts from God . . .

. . . school . . .

School Entrance

. . . Like music . . .

But above all this God has given us the gift of life, which is the most precious and wonderful gift. Like the little boy and his lunch, we may sometimes feel that we do not have much to give Jesus.

We may not be the fastest . . .

or most clever . . .

or strongest . . . or have the biggest lunch . . .
but we can still give to Jesus our gifts and our lives, after all . . .

John Ch.6 v47 & 48 → Follow the bread rolls and fill in the missing **Letters** to find out more about how Jesus calls Himself the bread that God has given

v47
'I am
_ e _ _ _ _ _ n _ you
the _ r _ _ _ _ :

... he who
_ e _ _ _ _ v _ _ _
has _ t _ _ _ _ _ _ _
life.

v48
I am the
_ _ e _ _ of _ _ i _ _

Colour In Pages

National Distributors

UK: (and countries not listed below)
CWR, Waverley Abbey House, Waverley Lane, Farnham, Surrey GU9 8EP.
Tel: (01252) 784700 Outside UK +44 (0)1252 784700

AUSTRALIA: CMC Australasia, PO Box 519, Belmont, Victoria 3216.
Tel: (03) 5241 3288

CANADA: Cook Communications Ministries, PO Box 98, 55 Woodslee Avenue, Paris, Ontario.
Tel: 1800 263 2664

GHANA: Challenge Enterprises of Ghana, PO Box 5723, Accra.
Tel: (021) 222437/223249 Fax: (021) 226227

HONG KONG: Cross Communications Ltd, 1/F, 562A Nathan Road, Kowloon.
Tel: 2780 1188 Fax: 2770 6229

INDIA: Crystal Communications, 10-3-18/4/1, East Marredpalli, Secunderabad – 500026. Andhra
Pradesh, Tel/Fax: (040) 27737145

KENYA: Keswick Books and Gifts Ltd, PO Box 10242, Nairobi.
Tel: (02) 331692/226047 Fax: (02) 728557

MALAYSIA: Salvation Book Centre (M) Sdn Bhd, 23 Jalan SS 2/64, 47300 Petaling Jaya, Selangor.
Tel: (03) 78766411/78766797 Fax: (03) 78757066/78756360

NEW ZEALAND: CMC Australasia, PO Box 36015, Lower Hutt.
Tel: 0800 449 408 Fax: 0800 449 049

NIGERIA: FBFM, Helen Baugh House, 96 St Finbarr's College Road, Akoka, Lagos.
Tel: (01) 7747429/4700218/825775/827264

PHILIPPINES: OMF Literature Inc, 776 Boni Avenue, Mandaluyong City.
Tel: (02) 531 2183 Fax: (02) 531 1960

REPUBLIC OF IRELAND: Scripture Union, 40 Talbot Street, Dublin 1.
Tel: (01) 8363764

SINGAPORE: Armour Publishing Pte Ltd, Block 203A Henderson Road, 11–06 Henderson Industrial
Park, Singapore 159546.
Tel: 6 276 9976 Fax: 6 276 7564

SOUTH AFRICA: Struik Christian Books, 80 MacKenzie Street, PO Box 1144, Cape Town 8000.
Tel: (021) 462 4360 Fax: (021) 461 3612

SRI LANKA: Christombu Books, 27 Hospital Street, Colombo 1.
Tel: (01) 433142/328909

TANZANIA: CLC Christian Book Centre, PO Box 1384, Mkwepu Street, Dar es Salaam.
Tel/Fax (022) 2119439

USA: Cook Communications Ministries, PO Box 98, 55 Woodslee Avenue, Paris, Ontario, Canada.
Tel: 1800 263 2664

ZIMBABWE: Word of Life Books, Shop 4, Memorial Building, 35 S Machel Avenue, Harare.
Tel: (04) 781305 Fax: (04) 774739

For email addresses, visit the CWR website: www.cwr.org.uk

CWR is a registered charity – number 294387

Titles in this series

Remember The Wise and Foolish Builders

ISBN: 1-85345-303-X

Remember The Good Samaritan

ISBN: 1-85345-301-3

Remember The Lost Sheep

ISBN: 1-85345-302-1

Remember When Jesus Walked on the Sea

ISBN: 1-85345-362-5

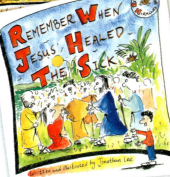
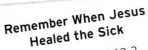

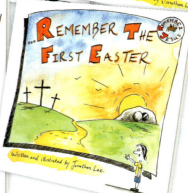

Remember When Jesus Healed the Sick

ISBN: 1-85345-363-3

Remember The First Christmas

ISBN: 1-85345-317-X

Remember The First Easter

ISBN: 1-85345-330-7

All books £3.99 each (plus p&p)

Prices correct at time of printing